EXPLORING WORLD CULTURES

Sri Lanka

Laura L. Sullivan

Cavendish
Square

New York

Published in 2020 by Cavendish Square Publishing, LLC
243 5th Avenue, Suite 136, New York, NY 10016

Library of Congress Cataloging-in-Publication Data

Names: Sullivan, Laura L., 1974- author.
Title: Sri Lanka / Laura L. Sullivan.
Description: First edition. | New York : Cavendish Square, 2020. |
Series: Exploring world cultures | Includes bibliographical references and index.
Identifiers: LCCN 2018052587 (print) | LCCN 2018053797 (ebook) | ISBN 9781502647214 (ebook) |
ISBN 9781502647207 (library bound) | ISBN 9781502647184 (pbk.) | ISBN 9781502647191 (6 pack)
Subjects: LCSH: Sri Lanka--Juvenile literature.
Classification: LCC DS489 (ebook) | LCC DS489 .S855 2020 (print) | DDC 954.93--dc23
LC record available at https://lccn.loc.gov/2018052587

Editorial Director: David McNamara
Editor: Lauren Miller
Copy Editor: Nathan Heidelberger
Associate Art Director: Alan Sliwinski
Designer: Christina Shults
Production Coordinator: Karol Szymczuk
Photo Research: J8 Media

The photographs in this book are used by permission and through the courtesy of:
Cover Dave Stamboulis/Alamy Stock Photo; p. 5 thekoala/iStockphoto.com; p. 6 Pavalena/ Shutterstock.com; p. 7 Goldream/iStock/Getty Images; p. 8 Peter Stuckings/Getty Images; p. 9 Sanjeewa Padmal Punchihewa/Wikimedia Commons/File:Sri Lankan Traditional Medicine.jpg/Public Domain; p. 10 Bryan R. Smith/AFP/Getty Images; p. 11 Ishara S. Kodikara/AFP/Getty Images; p. 12 Iren Key/Shutterstock.com; p. 13 Lakruwan Wanniarachchi/AFP/Getty Images; p. 14 Hadynyah/Getty Images; p. 16 Hadynyah/Getty Images; p. 18 Iryna Rasko/Shutterstock.com; p. 19 Steve Allen/ Shutterstock.com; p. 20 Saman Weeratunga/Shutterstock.com; p. 21 Saiko3p/Shutterstock.com; p. 22 John W Banagan/ Lonely Planet Images/Getty Images; p. 24 Thomas Wyness/Shutterstock.com; p. 25 Indrajith Embuldeniya/iStockphoto. com; p. 26 Ishara S. Kodikara/AFP/Getty Images; p. 28 F. Kavinda/Shutterstock.com; p. 29 Photosr4life/Shutterstock.com.

Printed in the United States of America

Contents

Introduction

Sri Lanka is a nation with a long history. It has many different people living there. The people come from many different places. They believe different things. Sometimes, these beliefs have led to fights. From 1983 to 2009, Sri Lanka went through a civil war.

Today, the war is over. The country is recovering. Business is growing and education is improving. Sri Lankan women have different roles too. Some have jobs in business and politics. In fact, Sri Lanka was the first country in the world to elect a female leader.

Sri Lanka is home to interesting animals, exciting cities, and historic places. People from around the world visit each year. There are old temples to see, beautiful beaches to walk, and delicious foods to eat.

Sri Lanka is a fascinating country to explore!

Sri Lanka is a mix of big cities like Colombo, pictured here, and beautiful countryside.

Sri Lanka is an island country just south of India. It is in the Indian Ocean. Once, there was a natural land bridge between Sri Lanka and India. However, it is not there anymore.

Sri Lanka is surrounded by many bodies of water.

The island is mostly flat. The only mountainous area is in the south-central part of the country. The

FACT!

Sri Lanka is usually hot, but in the mountains it can get cold.

Mangrove Trees

Mangrove trees are small and grow in salt water. They grow along the coast of Sri Lanka. These trees help protect the island from hurricanes and **tsunamis.**

As of 2015, all mangrove trees in Sri Lanka are protected by the government.

highest point is a mountain called Pidurutalagala. It is 8,281 feet (2,524 meters) tall.

Sri Lanka has long coastlines. It also has more than one hundred rivers. Many of these rivers have beautiful waterfalls. The weather in Sri Lanka is very warm and wet. Heavy rains called monsoons happen every year.

Throughout history, many different groups have ruled Sri Lanka. Ancient Sri Lankan kingdoms traded spices like cinnamon with Rome and medieval Europe.

This fort was built by the Dutch when they ruled Sri Lanka.

Later, Europeans took over the island. The Portuguese controlled the country during the 1600s. Then the Dutch ruled

FACT!

Sri Lanka's Queen Anula of Anuradhapura was the first woman to rule an Asian country. She reigned from 47 to 42 BCE.

The World's First Hospital

The first hospital in the world was in Sri Lanka. It was in use during the 300s BCE.

What is left of the world's first hospital

during the 1700s. Finally, the British took over in 1796 and called the island Ceylon.

The Sri Lankan people rebelled against the British. The country became independent in 1948. However, it was still under the influence of the British government until 1972.

Then there was a civil war from 1983 to 2009. A group called the Tamil Tigers fought for an independent Tamil country. They did not succeed.

Government

In 1931, Sri Lanka became the first **democracy** in Asia. It is still a democracy today.

Maithripala Sirisena became president of Sri Lanka in 2015.

The Sri Lankan government has three parts: executive, legislative, and judicial. The president leads the executive part. He or she serves for five years. He or she also appoints advisors called cabinet ministers.

FACT!

Sirimavo Bandaranaike became the world's first female elected leader when she became prime minister of Sri Lanka in 1960.

The parliament makes up the legislative part. Members of parliament are also elected for five-year terms. They make the country's laws. The parliament is headed by a

The parliament complex in Colombo

prime minister. Finally, the judicial part includes the Supreme Court, the Appeals Court, and several lower courts.

The president is in charge of the military. The Sri Lankan military fought during the civil war. Today, the military keeps peace throughout the country.

Voting Age

In Sri Lanka, everyone over the age of eighteen has the right to vote.

Sri Lanka's economy has changed throughout history. First, farming was most important to Sri Lanka. Until the mid-1800s, **plantations** grew many crops.

A worker harvests tea on a plantation in Hatton, Sri Lanka.

Crops like tea, rubber, and cinnamon were sold around the world. They helped Sri Lanka earn money. These crops are still grown today, but farming is not as important.

FACT!

Sri Lanka is one of the biggest producers of tea in the entire world.

Factories in Sri Lanka process food or make clothing.

Cinnamon comes from small trees.

The Sri Lankan economy struggled for many years. Today, it is improving. More people are making more money. Most homes have electricity and running water. However, the country is heavily in **debt**.

Other countries are helping Sri Lanka's economy grow. They trade with Sri Lanka.

Finding Work Opportunities

Many people from Sri Lanka go to the Middle East to work. They send money back to their families in Sri Lanka. The money helps the Sri Lankan economy.

The Environment

Sri Lanka has many plants and animals. There are many areas that try to protect them. Nature parks and **nature preserves** are examples. Animals like leopards, elephants, and macaque monkeys live there.

In Sri Lanka, some elephants are wild and some elephants work.

FACT!

Sri Lanka is at risk because of **climate change**. In the future, rising sea levels could harm coastal communities and businesses.

Sri Lanka has a lot of forests. Animals like sloth bears and crested serpent eagles live there. However, people want to cut the forests down because wood is valuable. It can make houses and other goods. Along the coast, shrimp farming threatens mangrove trees. Shrimp farms also harm coral reefs in the sea.

Today, many Sri Lankans drive cars and trucks. The vehicles cause a lot of air pollution. In the countryside, people litter and make the land and water dirty.

The Danger of Fires

Many people use firewood for cooking and heating. The ash and chemicals from burning wood cause pollution and health problems.

The People Today

More than twenty-two million people live in Sri Lanka. Most people live near the capital city of Colombo.

Sri Lanka is home to people of many different cultures.

Different groups live in Sri Lanka. The Sinhalese make up about 75 percent of the population. They mostly live in the central and southern parts of the country.

Sri Lankan descendants of people who came from Europe are called Burghers.

Similarities

The Sinhalese and Tamils have differences in culture, religion, and language. However, they have similar **genes**. Their ancestors probably came from the same area.

Sri Lankan Tamils make up about 11 percent of the population. They mostly live in the north of the country.

Sri Lankan Moors are another group. They make up about 9 percent.

Tamils from India and Malays also inhabit the island. There is a small group of Vedda people. They are related to the first people that lived in Sri Lanka.

Lifestyle

Family is important in Sri Lanka. Often, several generations live together. Traditionally, the father or the oldest son is considered the head of the

Tuktuks help people get around in cities.

family. Grandparents and other elderly people also live with family members. They are very respected.

Education is also important in Sri Lanka. About 92 percent of adults and 98 percent of

Instead of taxis, Sri Lankans use open, three-wheeled vehicles called *tuktuks*.

children know how to read. Education is free. Children have to go to school for at least nine years. However, only about 5 percent of people go to universities.

Many Sri Lankan families are big and close.

Both men and women work. In the past, men were the leaders and workers, while women stayed at home with the children. Today, more women are working, and more men are helping in their homes and with their children.

Marriage Traditions

In rural areas, there are still some arranged marriages. However, most Sri Lankans choose whom they marry.

Religion

There are many religions in Sri Lanka. People in Sri Lanka can practice any religion they want. Around 70 percent of Sri Lankans are Buddhist. They follow the teachings of the Buddha.

This is the Temple of the Tooth in Kandy, Sri Lanka.

Buddha was a monk who wanted to help end suffering. Most Sinhalese are Buddhist.

Roughly 12 percent of Sri Lankans are Hindu. Most of them are Tamil.

FACT!

There is a special temple called the Temple of the Tooth. It was built to house a tooth of Buddha.

Places of Worship

There are many buildings where people practice their religion. Buddhists and Hindus have temples. Muslims have mosques. Christians have churches.

Islam came to Sri Lanka with Middle Eastern traders. Followers of Islam are called Muslims. Less than 10 percent of Sri Lankans are Muslim.

Hindus worship at beautiful temples like this one.

Christianity was brought to Sri Lanka by Europeans. The number of Christians in Sri Lanka is small.

21

Language

Many languages are spoken in Sri Lanka. Sinhalese and Tamil are the country's two main languages. Sinhalese has a special alphabet. In it, vowels and consonants are combined into one letter.

Important signs are written in Sinhalese, Tamil, and English.

Since India is close by, Indian newspapers written in Tamil are available in Sri Lanka.

Arabic in Sri Lanka

Muslims in Sri Lanka usually speak Sinhalese or Tamil. **Arabic** is used for religious ceremonies.

The Tamil language has eighteen consonants and twelve vowels. It is also spoken by groups in India, Singapore, and other countries.

Both Sinhalese and Tamil are used in schools. English is also spoken in Sri Lanka. It is typically used for business. About 10 percent of Sri Lankans speak English.

There are also languages in Sri Lanka that mix two or more languages. They are called creoles. Two examples are Creole Malay and Creole Portuguese.

Arts and Festivals

Sri Lanka has festivals and celebrations throughout the year. Buddhists and Hindus celebrate the new year in April. In July and August, Buddhists celebrate the Festival of

A decorated elephant marches during the Festival of the Tooth.

the Tooth. Dancers perform with whips and fire. Elephants are painted. They wear jewels and colorful fabrics.

FACT!

Martin Wikramasinghe was a famous Sri Lankan writer. His novel *Viragaya* is considered one of the best books ever written in Sinhalese.

In January, Tamils have a four-day festival thanking the sun god. In February or March, a festival honors the god of destruction and changes, Shiva.

Sri Lankan dancers wear beautiful traditional costumes.

Sri Lankans have special dances too. Some dancers wear big headdresses. Other dances are less formal. Drums are used in most dances and plays. Early drama started out as small shows in villages. Today, there are several major theaters in Sri Lanka.

Sri Lankan Film

Early Sri Lankan movies were musicals. They had songs and dances.

Fun and Play

People enjoy many activities in Sri Lanka. Cricket is the most popular sport. It is played with a ball and a bat. The men's national team won the Cricket World Cup in 1996.

A cricket match between Sri Lanka and India in 2015

Tennis, soccer, rugby, and track and field are also common sports in Sri Lanka. The country has won two Olympic medals. In 1948,

Volleyball is the official sport of Sri Lanka.

Water Sports

Since Sri Lanka is an island, locals and tourists go to the beaches. They can swim, boat, scuba dive, and surf.

Duncan White won a silver medal for the men's 400-meter hurdles. Susanthika Jayasinghe also won a silver medal for the women's 200-meter race in 2000.

Sri Lanka has two native forms of martial arts. They are called *angampora* (AHN-gahm-PU-ruh) and *cheena di* (CHEE-nar-DEE). Angampora is a type of hand-to-hand combat. Cheena di is a fighting style that began in China.

27

Food

Rice is very popular in Sri Lanka. It is often served with a curry. Curry is a spicy sauce. It is usually made with lamb, chicken, or fish. Vegetarian versions use lentils or potatoes.

Kiribath is often served with a spicy onion chili sauce.

    Kiribath (kee-REE-bat) is also common. Rice is cooked in coconut milk until it is very soft. Once cool, it can be cut

FACT!

Watalappam is a popular dessert. It is a pudding made of coconut milk, nuts, and spices.

Falooda

Falooda is a drink, dessert, and meal all in one. It is made from rose syrup, ice cream, sweet basil seeds, noodles, and jelly.

Falooda is a sweet and colorful dessert.

into squares and eaten for breakfast. It is also served at festivals.

Street food is available in most cities in Sri Lanka. Snacks like fried rice, Chinese egg rolls, spicy mutton rolls, and fish or vegetable wraps are sold. People can eat them for breakfast or dinner.

29

Glossary

Arabic   A language from the Arabian Peninsula in the Middle East.

climate change   An increase in temperatures around the world due to pollution.

debt   Owing money to another person or group.

democracy   A government where representatives are elected by the people.

genes   The part of a cell that controls which traits are passed down from parents to children.

nature preserves   An area filled with plants and animals that is protected by the government.

plantation   A kind of large farm that grows one crop, tended by workers who live on-site.

tsunamis   Huge waves caused by an earthquake.

Find Out More

Books

Meister, Cari. *Do You Really Want to Meet an Elephant?* Mankato, MN: Amicus, 2016.

O'Brien, Cynthia. *Cultural Traditions in Sri Lanka*. New York: Crabtree, 2017.

Website

Ducksters: Sri Lanka

https://www.ducksters.com/geography/country.php?country=Sri%20Lanka

Video

Sri Lanka Travel Guide

https://www.youtube.com/watch?v=epmQYVLvnjU

This video hits the highlights of Sri Lanka with an engaging tour guide to show off the sights.

Index

About the Author

Laura L. Sullivan is the author of more than forty fiction and nonfiction books for children, including the fantasies *Under the Green Hill* and *Guardian of the Green Hill*. She lives in Florida where she likes to bike, hike, kayak, hunt fossils, and practice Brazilian jiujitsu.